# A THREE DAYS' JOURNEY

by

Margaret B Doll

*To Suzanne with love,*
*Margaret Doll*

*To my husband,*

*Jim*

# *PREFACE*

Throughout history God has used his servants to exhort his people to remember the things he has done. For if we forget the past, the danger is not that we repeat it, but that we forget the one who is working out his plan of redemption on our behalf and for the honor of his name. But the cares of the world crowd in and rob God of the honor due him. The world beckons us away from him…towards our own man made idols. Little by little the ideas and philosophies of the world have challenged God's word unrelentingly. In the spirit of analysis and scrutiny, the educated and intellectuals still echo the words so long ago spoken, 'Did God really say…?" Can the Scriptures be trusted? Aren't they just stories? Doesn't science take precedence?

God called Moses to lead his people out of Egypt. All they needed was a three days' journey to get far enough away form the cultic practices and influence of that nation so that they could celebrate a festival to God and worship him. In this era, people are still in need of finding a place uninfluenced by the world, a spiritual place where they can worship in spirit and in truth.

Three is a significant biblical number. Three is the minimum number needed to establish a pattern; it serves as a rhetorical signal indicating significance; biblical episodes that occur in sequences of three often generate a sense of expectation; once an event has occurred for the third time, something new and unexpected is likely to happen; three speaks of totality and sufficiency and connotes completeness.

A Three Days' Journey is an invitation to rediscover our identity in Christ, the unity he calls us to for the honor of his name, and the sense of worship that comes from knowing him and loving him with all our hearts and minds. It is a book written in a narrative style but rich in theological truths embedded in everyday contexts. And hopefully it will establish a pattern of trust in God's word,

significance in being made in his image, a joyous and hopeful

expectation of his return, and a sense of completeness that comes

only from truly knowing, loving, and leaning on him.

# INTRODUCTION

## Genesis 5-11

*According to the book of Genesis chapter seven, Noah was six hundred years old when the flood of waters came upon the earth. Noah was eight hundred and ninety-two years old when Abram was born to Terah. When Noah died at the age of nine hundred and fifty, Abram was fifty-eight years old. Abram, who was a direct descendant of Noah's son, Shem, might have known both Noah and Shem.*

*Noah would have known Methuselah, who died before the flood at the age of nine hundred and sixty-nine. Methuselah, the son of Enoch who was three hundred and fifty-six years old when he "was no more, because God took him away," would have known Adam,* because Adam would have still been alive for two hundred and fifty years after Methuselah was born.

The history of creation, the banishment from the garden, and the great flood would have been preserved through oral tradition, and accessible to Abram.

In fact, Abram's story might have begun something like this . . .

# PROLOGUE

"Indeed, I will bring forth in shining light those who loved
my holy name,
and I will seat each one on the throne of his honor,
and they will shine for times without number.
For righteous is the judgment of God,
and to the faithful he shows faithfulness,
because they abide in the paths of truth."
1 Enoch 108: 12-13

*Mesopotamia, 1755 B.C.*

Abram leaned in closer and listened as the ancient patriarch struggled to speak. His words came slowly and with great effort, "Remember . . . remember . . . remember the words of the wise." He coughed slightly, struggling to breathe. Abram barely heard him as he managed to finish, saying, "They will be saved." He breathed his last, and as the sun flickered in through the slightly parted opening to the tent entrance, a gentle lifting of the breeze seemed to confirm that he had left this earth and departed to a better place.

As Abram returned home to Haran, after the period of mourning, he thought about all that his ancient father, Noah, had taught him. How was it that humankind had wandered so far from the creator? How easily they forget . . . or rather, how occupied they become with their own endeavors that they do not listen to the words of the wise ones. Abram had heard Noah speak the words of Enoch many times. He knew them well . . . "Blessed will be all who listen to the words of the wise, and learn to do the commandments of the Most High; and walk in the paths of his righteousness, and do not err with the erring; for they will be saved."[1] But the tendencies of humankind always led to erring, and though the flood brought the possibility of new beginnings, it had not taken long for the words of the wise to be crowded out with the ways of the world.

Abram's own father, Terah, had become a man too distracted and pre-occupied with the world to listen to the words of the wise. His collection of carved images to which he offered daily worship attested to that. "There are many gods," his father had angrily shouted at him one day as Abram questioned him about these gods of stone and wood. "You had better listen to me! All humankind must acknowledge them or live in fear of their power," he warned.

Abram listened well . . . better than his father gave him credit. And he remembered. He remembered that there had been a time when people had gathered as one to claim proprietorship over the god of all gods, to meet him and offer obeisance to him, eye to eye. They built a city with a tower that would reach into the very dwelling place of the high god; not for the glory of his name, but so that their name would be great on the earth.

But the tower was never finished. In His mercy the Creator put a stop to their arrogant effort rather than destroy them. The people were dispersed, unable to communicate with one another any longer. They spread across the earth, all of them after their own gods, after their own pursuits and pleasures. Their plan had been a masterful undertaking. It would have been the pinnacle of human accomplishment – a magnificent city with a temple tower for the god of gods to reside, and for humankind to achieve all they desired. Oh, how they had forgotten! Would they make a name for themselves? Would they achieve greatness in their fallen state and command the Almighty? Were we not all banished from that which was perfect because of our self-will and rebellion? Was it not told about in the Song of Remembrance?

But they did not want to remember. In their own strength and self -sufficiency they sought to live their lives apart from the shame they inherited. Little by little the truth was suppressed, and the ancient story of origins was changed. Even the story about the Creator's judgment of humankind that brought about the flood was changed. Was it because the truth was too painful? Whatever the reason, the words were translated into something else, something that fit new languages with new beginnings.

Who would have thought that the very means the creator used in creation, the gift of speech given to humankind for worship and fellowship, would become a vehicle for deception? But long ago the great enemy had used words to cast doubt and deceive the first man and woman when he proposed, "Did God really say . . . ?" They never forgot the painful result of their foolish choice when they listened to the deceiver instead of being obedient to the Most High God. With tears and great shame they told their sons and daughters of the consequence of that moment. "Listen and remember," they said over and over. "He will send a Redeemer," they reminded each of their descendants, their countenance filled with hope.

Their stories were wondrous and frightening; creation and order by the very word of God; a vast universe of stars beyond count; an earth filled with diverse creatures over and upon the land and in the waters; the man created from the dust of the earth and the woman taken from his side, both made in the image of the Creator to rule together over all the earth; a garden with all they would ever want or need. Then in a moment of rebellion they conceived sin; and with it came shame, fear, banishment, separation, pain and toil. Seth listened and remembered, and with him many of the sons and daughters began to call on the name of the Lord. Enoch listened and proclaimed aloud to all, the beginning from the end . . . and then he was taken to be with the Creator, God Most High. His son Methuselah listened well.

And then during Noah's time came the flood. He had been the only one of the ancients left who still called on the name of the Lord. And with him the stories of our ancestors were kept safe from the waters of chaos that engulfed the whole earth.

And yet, Enoch's words spoke of another saving. What could it mean? The earth was already full of wickedness again, especially the cities, where the gods carved of wood and stone reigned. Perhaps the truth was too painful. But still, it was the truth.

Abram shook his head in sorrow as he thought on all of these things. He directed his remaining strength toward his long journey home. Abram had no love for Haran. He wiped his brow against the penetrating heat of the day and his thoughts turned to softer, kinder images as his beautiful Sarai came to mind, and he smiled as he anticipated his return to the one who could comfort him now.

## Part One

## Bring My People Out

### Invictus

*It matters not how strait the gate,
How charged with punishments the scroll,
I am the master of my fate:
I am the captain of my soul.*

William Ernest Henley

# 1

*Camden, South Carolina. 2009 A.D.*

Amidst much gaiety and camaraderie, Stephen stood and offered a toast to our host and founder of the School of Public Speaking, finishing with a short but memorable impromptu speech. Then, with wit and aplomb, Stephen announced that each of the students would stand and give their regards, accolades, and some words of retrospection on the last few days.

My heart began to pound . . . what was he thinking? He was obviously proportionately inspired by the amount of wine he had consumed. I frantically scanned my brain for something clever to say as Stephen called on names, one by one. After the third person, I heard my name called. My heart was pounding and I was feeling suffocated. I wanted to crawl under the table, feign sickness, anything but stand up and make an impromptu speech. This wasn't part of the course – I had not prepared.

The evening had been so enjoyable up to this point. We were all dressed up for this closing dinner; ten students, five instructors, our host and his lovely wife, and the two newspaper reporters who had helped in the course by drilling each of us before a camera so that we could see ourselves and do a critique. Also in attendance was the camera and recording team, and the woman who helped us get over our speaking inhibitions by making us do a session of foolish activities to loosen up our faces, mouths, and hands. We were spread out at several tables that were still laden with the remains of our dessert and coffee. The attendees had enjoyed cocktails, conversation, and a wonderful dinner. But I would gladly decline this pousse-café.

I knew no excuse would suffice, though; there was no escape. I had not had enough wine to sound witty to myself, and all that came to mind was a story I had recently heard a few weeks ago, for the second time. So, smiling, I stood up, and trying to look and sound confident, began.

"I watched the movie, *Catch Me if You Can*, a few weeks ago for the second time." Everyone waited in anticipation of something clever to follow. "In it, the father of the main character stands up early in the film while at an awards dinner and tells the story of two mice. 'Two mice fell into a vat of cream. One mouse swam and swam in circles until he churned that cream into butter and climbed out. I am that mouse.' The audience applauded loudly, recognizing that here was a man who had overcome obstacles, and through his own wherewithal had succeeded where anyone else may have failed."

I did not want to think too much about what I was about to say next. I was pretty sure it would not be easily perceived without undo processing, which no one seemed to be in the mood to exercise at this point in the dinner. However, I ventured forward.

"Well, I am the other mouse, the one that drowned. But an invisible hand reached down into the vat and pulled me out and gave me a new life."

I smiled valiantly, then offered a few words about not being the successful self-made person our culture idolizes, but relying instead on the Lord to guide and direct, even to the point of Him making it possible for me to attend the School of Public Speaking. I pointed out what an honor and wonderful opportunity it had been, gave the proper thank you to the host and founder, and confidently took my seat. There was the polite amount of applause as the next student was called upon to give his stand-up speech. Recovering, I analyzed what I had just shared. My audience for those brief attentive moments was probably baffled . . . maybe each thinking they had missed something important, something profound that was the key to understanding my *story*.

Glad to be out of the spotlight and hoping that the next student had something memorable enough to say that my speech would be quickly forgotten or filed away for further processing at a later date, I tucked my curdled cream story away. I was not sure it had made an impact on this audience. Here was a room full of people who had come together for a workshop to learn and exercise the fine art of how to speak in public and triumphantly persuade and win an audience. They were successful leaders in their communities and businesses. A mouse drowning in cream and being lifted out by the hand of deity was probably not the story to tell. But, there, I had done it. And I really did hope that someone in the room would take the time to think about it.

2

The next morning as I made the hour and a half drive home, I reflected on the self-made person so admired in our Western culture. I was raised in an environment that honored and respected independence and self-sufficiency. One of my father's favorite poems was *Invictus*, by William Ernest Henley. He especially liked Henley's line on being "the master of my fate . . . the captain of my soul." As a teenager who had become what some labeled "fiercely independent," I had let that line out as far as I could before it snapped and I found myself in a world with no absolute up or down. Yep, I was the mouse that did not climb out of the milk vat. I was lifted out and given new life. And I had found that being dependent on God was a very good place to be.

Arriving home, my husband wanted to hear all about the workshop. So I poured out the wows and woes of the last three days.

"I'm glad I stayed for the whole thing," I admitted to him. "But to tell you the truth, after the first day I was really tempted to come home."

"What happened?" he asked, concerned and surprised by my response.

"Well, I didn't realize we were going to have to research a political incident, write a paper on it, and then take one or the other side in a group debate. I'm glad I at least knew something about the issue. And I was put on the side that represented my perspective. But I was so tired after the first day and the idea of doing all that reading, and writing a paper defending a perspective as my evening assignment, it was just too much at the end of a long day."

He looked at me sympathetically. "What else went on? What else did you do?" he asked, hoping I had something more positive to report.

I told him about the interviews we had to do with the reporters and some of the other sessions that prepared us to be able to navigate various public speaking situations.

"I had a chance to talk about the work we do with our mission organization," I told him, enthusiastically. "One of our sessions involved being interviewed by a reporter. He questioned me about my work and I was able to talk about the various cultures we work with, the need to address those language groups that are oral communicators, and how we help translation teams by providing media resources and tools for communicating the stories of the Bible. In fact, at the dinner on the final evening one of the instructors asked me how Bible stories would be able to carry theological truths. I reminded her that Jesus' parables did just that."

My husband seemed pleased that the workshop had gone well, and was even happier that I was back home. Wanting to share the grand finale of the dinner on the final evening in a nonchalant way, I added, "Yes, the dinner last night was really nice except that before it was over one of the attendees got the bright idea to have each of us stand up and give an impromptu speech, a sort of final word to sum up our experience and display our newly acquired skill. It took me by surprise ... I didn't know what to say, and when my name was called all I could think to do was share about the story from the movie, *Catch Me If You Can*; the one the father tells at the beginning about the two mice that fell in the vat of cream."

My husband's eyes narrowed and he looked at me skeptically, waiting to hear more. "It was probably not the story to tell that group, but it was all that came to my mind and I had to think of something to share, and quickly. But that story really captures the way people in our culture idolize those who 'make it on their own.' Everyone admires the self-sufficient person. I know the whole concept came from the work ethic and sense of individualism that was, in part, due to the Reformation. But God has been taken out of the equation for so many people. You know how my dad loved the poem, *Invictus*. It captures his ethical worldview of taking charge of your own life. It's not that Dad refused to acknowledge a dependency on God. I think he, like most of modern Western mankind, just lost touch with making the reality of the presence of and dependency on God a part of daily life. People have just forgotten the history behind their identity."

I told Joe about the comments I made after my story . . . about me being the mouse that drowned but was rescued and revived to live again.

I could tell Joe was trying to imagine the scenario in his mind, his wife standing up at a dinner event and telling the story of two mice who fell in a vat of cream, albeit with an unexpected ending. He sort of shook his head, unable to quite picture it, and looked at me with a mixture of incredulity and pride.

"Yea," I said, "somehow I got through the thing. I'm just glad to be home!"

# 3

Later that evening, Joe and I resumed our conversation about modern Western man (I was glad he didn't bring up my mouse story). We discussed modern man's quest for social utopia and the thinking that fueled that idea. We also talked about the continued quest for world peace and economic stability built on education, equality, and mutual respect for diverse worldviews.

"The thinking is that somehow mankind can achieve peace and prosperity," Joe mused.

"Ah yes . . . utopia, the perennial heresy; the idea that somehow mankind can regain the garden of paradise; that mankind can achieve completion, unity, cohesion," I pondered aloud.

"Yes, its funny, isn't it? Long ago in ancient times people gathered together in a united effort to build the tower of Babel, as a sort of monument to themselves; an achievement to make a name for themselves. And now thousands of years later people are still trying to make a name for themselves, to create a grand unified society by their own hand, a sort of organized effort to bring peace and prosperity; a utopia on earth. Only now there are thousands of language groups in the world and as many worldviews, with major cultural differences."

"And the utopian uses the language of unity and community but has a distorted idea that this means a kind of uniformity that renounces individual freedom, one where everything is equal with everything else," Joe reflected.

"The thing is, for Christians there is a unity to be had, our unity in Christ. And we all need to remember that it wasn't accomplished by anything we did, but by God himself, and at great cost," I added.

"But even Christians struggle to get along. They don't behave like they have any kind of unity," Joe reminded me. "I work with people who are difficult, and this is in a work environment made up of people who are believers and are serving the Lord in the very work they are doing."

"That reminds me of a quote I once read that goes something like, 'The most important aspect of Christianity is not the work we do, but the relationship we maintain and the surrounding influence and qualities produced by that relationship. That is all God asks us to give our attention to, and it is the one thing that is continually under attack.'"2

"Yes, I agree," Joe nodded. "Our work for the Lord can sometimes take priority over the relationships we have with those we work with. We allow it to take priority. It shouldn't be that way, but it often is."

"Well, that whole thing about work being a priority over relationships is in part a Western cultural disposition. As Westerners, we have had it ingrained in our minds that we should work as unto the Lord. After the Reformation, the concept was that Christians were all part of the priesthood of believers and any work they did was valuable to the Lord, just like it says in the New Testament. So people began to work diligently as a way of honoring the Lord. And I think the work began to take priority over relationships. Oh, I am sure that there were many other things that contributed. In fact, the anthropologist, Edward Hall, says that the linear thinking patterns that were fostered by literacy and education have stifled comprehensive ways of thinking and promoted individualism. [3] And there was a study done that showed that Western societies are very "performance" oriented; they value results from one's work more than people."[4]

Joe got a funny distant kind of look, and then said, "I just realized something."

"What's that?" I asked, curious about the enlightened look on his face.

"Your mouse story . . ." he started to say.

"Oh no," I thought. I wasn't ready to be reminded of that just now.

"I bet your mouse story would have been very hard for a non-westerner to process!"

"Hmm," I mumbled, "I guess so. If the mice had been non-westerners they would have worked together to get out of their situation. But the one mouse thought only of himself, and in the process of churning the cream into butter he buried his little friend."

We both laughed as we imagined the scenario and the revelation it gave to the cultural value of work over relationships.

"Well," Joe added, "despite the conflicts I sometimes observe, I know the people I work with really love the Lord and want to honor Him. I think He is doing as much work in each of us as we are doing for Him."

"That reminds me of an interesting conversation I had with one of our colleagues who works in a country in Africa. She directs a multi-cultural team and so has had to navigate lots of different perceptions her team members have about how she should lead. She also has to help them navigate the cultural differences on their team. But she told me a story that has helped her through a lot of difficult situations and has given her a better perspective on her work and relationships."

"Ah, another story on the schemes of mice and men?"[5] Joe chuckled, sarcastically.

"Nope, this one actually shows that God is at work is all aspects of our lives. And, as a matter of fact, I know a few other stories of people working in difficult situations who turned to God when they could not understand their circumstances," I said.

"You mean like Joseph, Esther, Daniel, and others from the Bible?"

"Well, yes, in a way . . . It's their experiences and example that help remind us."

"We always need reminders, don't we? It is easy to forget."

Joe breathed loudly as he shook his head.

So I told Joe about Alice.

4

Alice and I were having a conversation about her experiences in her leadership position and I had asked her to tell me about some of the incidents that she had that might help others who are working in a cross-cultural context.

"When I first worked in Africa it was in a missionary health clinic with an African staff. I didn't know much about cultural differences then, other than what was obvious. I learned the hard way that some differences only show up in certain circumstances. We had a wonderful garden on the clinic property, lots of fruit and nut trees. But we wanted to build a shelter, so we cut down some of the trees. We had a lot of leftover wood we didn't need and I suggested we let everyone on staff have some of it to use as firewood. I soon found out that I had made a big mistake. It turns out that in African culture, if you planted the tree, you own the tree. And the African woman, who had planted the trees in the clinic garden as a youth, thirty years ago, considered those trees hers. She had worked with the missionaries at the clinic as a young girl and had planted the seeds of those trees. They were cashew trees, very valuable since the nut can be used as money, and the fruit is very precious. We had cut down the trees without her permission.

"So a meeting was called at the church, a serious meeting to discuss the wrongdoing. I became the center of focus because I had suggested everyone share the leftover wood. But the woman was thinking, 'These are my trees, this is my wood.' So we sat at the church and they talked and talked about the right and wrongs of it. Well, I became really emotional about it all and finally left the meeting, crying. Evidently, that was a turning point for the others who were still deeply engaged in the discussion. They continued on with the meeting, but acknowledged that I had not acted maliciously, but out of ignorance; and the lady who owned the wood forgave me. The church leadership helped bring about the reconciliation.

"I realized that my response was a Western response. I had been raised in India, had Indian parents, but as a teenager my family had relocated to England. So I had internalized a more Western worldview and cultural response. An African response would not be to cry; they would thrash it all out between themselves. But they realized the incident had really affected me emotionally. They had originally thought I was just being stubborn. I now know that the African lady was just looking for acknowledgement of the injustice of the whole thing. I was stressed and upset because I did not know how the whole thing could possibly be resolved. She was not expecting resolution so much as just simply an admission that what had been done was wrong, unjust.

"I am grateful that all who were involved were Christians. In the end, I was forgiven and everyone took a bit of the firewood and it all worked out. It was an emotional experience for me but I worked through it and learned something. And I found out that it is okay to be myself; I didn't have to be like them in order to resolve the situation. I learned that what we bring to a situation is valuable and important.

"Now I still work in Africa, and I still have a lot to learn about cultural differences. I also have a lot to learn about working with a multi-cultural team. I want my team to understand me, my leadership style, and also be aware of the differences among the team. My team needs to have resources that can help them understand cultural differences so they can get along with one another. You know, I was talking with my team about worldview one day. None of them had heard that term. I explained what it meant and how it affects one's cultural response. Well, they began to talk about how important relationships are to them in contrast to how many Westerners respond. I explained to them that relationships are important to me also, but that I show it differently. I explained that when I have to cut a conversation short because of another engagement, it is not that I don't think the conversation and relationship are important. It is that the other person is also important and that person is going to be waiting on me for a meeting we had planned and I don't want to be rude by not showing up at the time we agreed on. You know, when I explained myself to them they got it. Sometimes we are so quick to try and adapt to another culture without explaining to our colleagues from that culture why our perspective might be acceptable.

"We do have some serious cultural differences on our team, and I would really like the team members to get some training on major fundamental differences. But we realize we have to be dependent on the Lord in order to work together successfully, because our difficulties are not always just cultural differences; we also encounter a lot of spiritual battles. I appreciate some of the leadership over me and am encouraged because I know they are aware of their own dependence on God and they take time in their relationship with him and in the Word. They also are truly concerned for my team and me. And that speaks more to me than whether they are able to deal with various situations or not.

"We have learned together the importance of under-girding our work with prayer. We know we can expect conflict, but if prayer is our bottom line, God will win. In some of the most difficult situations, I am reminded of how much God loves the people we are serving here in this country. But I have learned something else. One afternoon after my quiet time and a short nap, I woke up feeling really refreshed. I reflected on how wonderful it was to be serving the Lord as a missionary. I was really patting myself on the back, you know, when God clearly spoke to me and said, 'Alice, I didn't bring you here to be a missionary . . . I brought you here because I have things in you I want to change. I am doing it here because this is the only place I can do it.' It made me realize that God is

concerned for what he's doing in me as well as through me."

# 5

After Alice shared her story I couldn't help but think about how much we all need to depend on the Lord in everything. I remembered the story about Moses when he encountered God at the burning bush and questioned God's directive to him to go and speak to Pharaoh on behalf of the Israelites so that they might be released from their slavery and freely worship God alone. Moses' response to God was, "Who am I that I should go to Pharaoh to bring the Israelites out of Egypt?" And God answered him saying, 'I will be with you." I realized it is not about who we are, but about who he is. And that was the start of God not only molding his people and teaching them about who he is, but molding Moses as their leader and helping him stay committed to the task.

Joe and I talked some more about Alice's story. We could see some interesting parallels.

"It's interesting, God is molding each of us. We are his people, his house, like living stones being built up. He is the architect and builder, and we are his temple. And he is also building unity in us," I reflected.

"Yes," Joe agreed. "To know Christ and to make his name known is a powerful and unifying purpose, despite cultural and theological differences."

"What's also interesting to think about is that utopians seek a kind of unification and they imagine they can achieve it by their own hand," I added. "The builders of the temple structure we know as the Tower of Babel, from the Old Testament, wanted to achieve a kind of solidarity and make a name for themselves. In ancient times, temple building always involved the mandate of the King in a time of peace, and gathering the materials and laying a foundation. And the interesting parallel there is that the New Testament says Christ has made peace through his blood which was shed on the cross, and that we are the materials, the living stones, and the foundation is the apostles and prophets, with Christ the cornerstone, God the builder."

"Where did you learn about temple building?" Joe asked.

"Well, I had that course, History and Archeology of the Ancient Near East," I reminded him. "But I also read an article recently by Brian Peterson, where he talks about the vision of a temple the Old Testament prophet Ezekiel had.[6] It was after the nation of Israel had gone into exile in Babylon and their temple in Jerusalem had been destroyed. Ezekiel has a vision of a new temple, but the new temple is already built. Ezekiel describes the edifice and its measurements, and apparently God uses the whole vision as a sort of reminder to Israel that they cannot truly know God unless they keep a permanent remembrance of what they were saved from and the graciousness of the salvation they have been given.

And Ezekiel tells the nation they must measure the temple plan and proportions as a reminder that God is building something new in which their hand had no part. It was supposed to be a way to shame them, but also to remind them of God's forgiveness. They were a 'shame and honor' society. They robbed God of his honor by their behavior that brought shame on themselves, and led to the demise of their temple. They violated the covenant and had not behaved in a way that reflected on the holiness of God and his temple. That is why they were given over to the Babylonians for a time of exile."

"Interesting," Joe said thoughtfully. "What do you know about shame and honor societies?"

"Well, a lot of the language groups our organization works with fall into that category. They are very community oriented, in contrast to Western individualism. In fact, that whole area of community oriented societies that are more focused on relationships, versus individualistic societies that are so task oriented, creates fertile ground for conflict in cross-cultural settings. This is especially evident where you have people working together on teams with team leaders whose cultural leadership style differs from the expectations of those on the team."

"I also had a chance to talk to another colleague, Ruth, about her experiences in a leadership position working in Southern Asia, I added. She managed to deal with the difficult situation of her expectations of leadership and her own leadership style by trusting the Lord. But I think it would help those in leadership working cross-culturally to have more information about cultural differences, so there can be a deeper understanding and better relationships with those who are working together."

Joe was worn out with the day and we decided to turn in for the night. "Tell me about Ruth tomorrow," he mumbled.

# Part Two

## The Lord God is Sovereign

### To A Mouse

*But little Mouse, you are not alone,*
*In proving foresight may be vain:*
*The best laid schemes of mice and men*
*Go often askew,*
*And leave us nothing but grief and pain,*
*For promised joy!*

Robert Burns
(English translation)

# 6

I had just asked Ruth about how she was managing her position in Southeast Asia and whether she had experienced any conflicts due to cultural differences.

"Yes," she answered, in her heavy French German accent. "My husband and I are from a country in Europe and so we have a different understanding about being a colleague or having a boss. One person I had to deal with was taking over my responsibilities. I did not think he needed to do that so I went straight to him and told him that I would handle my own responsibilities. I think he was shocked that I spoke to him the way I did. I wasn't angry, though. He was actually my supervisor and I do not think he thought I was doing my job very efficiently. After that encounter we did not speak much to each other. I prayed about it and decided to leave it with God. Maybe I was too outspoken."

"Did you ever get things resolved and worked out with him?" I asked Ruth.

"No, my husband and I just moved on. Our conclusion was that we had made a commitment to be in this country to do this work . . . a commitment to God. I decided that I would just be less outspoken, quieter, and go to prayer more and ask God to help us.

"There have been other conflicts, though, which have been much harder to adjust to," Ruth added.

"Tell me what you mean," I encouraged. I knew that for Ruth and her husband it must be a challenge to be from a culture that values and practices assertiveness and does not differentiate the roles of men and women, yet be working in a culture that does not value assertiveness and does differentiate gender roles. Being from a Germanic country in Europe, she was accustomed to being allowed to work autonomously. She was also used to a boss or supervisor who would allow her to work things out and empower and motivate her to do so. Her supervisor in this current position was a national from the host country. His behavior was not what she expected, and she had responded to him in a way that he had not expected, either. Surely he wasn't used to such directness, especially from a woman.

Ruth was also not from a "face saving" culture. I could understand why the conflict had not been resolved. Her supervisor would have expected Ruth to confide in an arbiter, they both knew and respected, and the arbiter would have worked to amend the conflict.

How hard it must be for a person with a cultural background that values job performance and assertiveness, and has a future-focused perspective that helps mitigate the uncertainties of life, to be living and working in a country that was so different, a country where people are not so direct in their communications.

So, I was surprised when Ruth told me what this "harder" conflict was.

"God is helping me adjust," she admitted. "I have learned to take everything to him in prayer. You see, we all know that the facility here where we work will be closing down soon. I have really come to love the people of this country, and it is hard to think about leaving. But those of us who work here are all praying more, and we are carrying the pain together. This helps us. My husband and I have no idea what we will do next, where we will go. But we have learned to react to challenges according to the Bible; we are letting God's grace control our response. We trust he will bring us to the right place where we can serve him in whatever capacity he allows."

I was surprised because I was expecting some personal conflict. What I heard was that Ruth was dealing with the uncertainty of the future. And she found comfort in the group effort of praying and carrying the pain together. She was losing her "home" at a time when she was comfortable with her work and with the people she was serving in the country. I remembered the story of Abraham, who was called by God to leave his home and go to a place he did not know. What a step of faith he made in obeying God and stepping out into a future of uncertainty in many respects. One thing he was certain of, though, was that it was God calling him. And God made some unique promises to him. He had to depend on God to do the directing, and much of what he was told to do was very difficult.

# 7

Joe listened to Ruth's story over breakfast and commented at the end, "I am really impressed with how Ruth handled the challenges she encountered. I wish I had been less grumpy about the many times we have had to move over the years. But I guess I have learned over time to trust the Lord with each day."

"For some of us it takes a little longer to really learn to trust God. Often we say we do, but when big changes occur that were not planned, we balk," I admitted. "Maybe it is a cultural response. I think most Westerners are very careful about planning for the future. And when things don't go the way we planned we feel anxious, sometimes angry; we don't handle it well. We like predictability and we work hard to avoid uncertainties."

"Well, you know what the Bible says . . . we are just sojourners here in this world. I guess we are not meant to get too comfortable," Joe added.

"And the Bible also says that though we make our plans, it is the Lord who will determine what we do. So we should always be aware of his plan for our lives and be flexible to the changes in direction that we encounter, knowing he is sovereign," I concluded.

"You know, it has been interesting getting to know the stories of some of my colleagues who are working cross-culturally. I mean, they don't always respond to their situations like they know they should, but at least they know when their responses or attitudes are not lining up with what God's Word says."

"That is true for the group I work with, too," Joe reflected. "We may not be dealing with cross-cultural issues so much, but we still deal with conflicts. I guess there will always be personality differences, and sometimes people are also dealing with other stresses that factor in to how they respond and treat one another. I really liked what Ruth said about the group carrying the pain together. I think, for the most part, we do that in my office. And I can see that what Alice said is true for all of us. God is working in each of us much more than we realize. We need to remember that."

"Joe, that reminds me of another story," I grinned at him.

"Okay, okay . . . you have an endless collection of stories, don't you! You have my attention but let's wait until after lunch. We have to get that wood cut, split and stacked before this weather front comes in. And I could really use your help!"

Joe and I worked outside, getting some large logs cut to fit the wood-burning stove. I did the heavy lifting because of his back problem, and he ran the chain saw. I helped position the logs so he could use the axe to split them. Sometimes we would find nests of ants or other bugs in the split logs, now disturbed and sluggishly waking up, only to be swished away by Joe's gloved hand and forced to seek another place to hibernate. We worked for a couple of hours, cutting, splitting and stacking the wood under the shelter Joe built. We put a good supply up on the back porch where Joe could easily get to it for keeping the wood stove going.

We finished our work before the cold front came in, and while Joe was doing maintenance on the chain saw I went in to start some lunch. Shortly after, Joe came in and added some logs to the fire in the stove. We were cozy and prepared for the bad weather.

While we ate our lunch I started the story that David had recently told me about his experiences with his Western colleagues working together in his home country in Sub-Sahara Africa.

# 8

David was serving in a leadership position in his own country of origin. He worked with colleagues who were from many other countries. Some of his colleagues had been working in his country for decades, sometimes working in remote villages and rarely coming into the major city. There always seemed to be a time warp between the traditions in the villages and the more modern lifestyles in the city. David was well aware of the differences and didn't give it much thought. But one day one of his Western colleagues, an elderly woman who had worked for many years out in the villages, noticed that he was holding hands with his wife. The woman called them over and explained to them that here in this country holding hands in public is unacceptable. David was a little taken aback. Why was this Western colleague telling him what was right and wrong in his own culture? He tried to explain the way things have changed in the culture but she wasn't buying it. He finally just dropped the issue.

"That must have been awkward," I said to David.

David looked at me with keen, thoughtful eyes, "Yes, it was awkward. But what has been even more awkward is the work environment with Africans and Westerners and others on staff," he admitted. "Africans like to socialize a lot – they come to work and want to greet one another. The Westerners come in and get right to work."

"I am sure that must make you think they don't want to build relationships," I suggested.

"I don't really think that," David said. "No, the thing that is difficult is that they seem to resent the fact that we take so much time away from work. But that's just our culture. I think they just don't really understand African culture. We need someone in leadership who can help our staff adjust to the cultural differences among us and make some allowances. For instance, some Westerners are very direct when they want to confront you. But in my country, we are more diplomatic. If someone comes to your house to visit you, you know that it is probably for something more than a social visit. But first you take the time to visit and establish the relationship, and then finally you bring up the problem or issue you need to talk about.

"There are other issues that need to be addressed by leadership but sometimes the person in leadership is not really qualified," David continued. They may be in the position only because of staff shortages and availability. Conflicts come up that interrupt our team attitude and even though we know the importance of working together as a team, we are not given good direction and things fester. It just seems like some people will never get along no matter what you do, even among our own culture. It takes so much out of you."

David and I talked a little further about other conflicts that came up and he admitted that at one time he thought becoming a Christian meant having one hundred percent protection and provision.

"I keep my feelings to myself," he confided. "Whether I am sad or whether I am happy, I don't express it. People interpret things so differently. I have learned to take advantage of today. God has used a number of circumstances to teach me that even a 'green' leaf can fall anytime.

"There are still many languages in my country and the surrounding countries that don't even have the start of a Bible translation project. Some of my national colleagues who are educated and well trained are eager to get out and train others and start working among these languages. But the expats are standing in the way. They know how to do the work but they are not allowing my colleagues to do the same work. I think they don't want to let go. Maybe they are afraid to make others equal. But why not train others? We could get the work done faster. They know they should be building capacity and empowering their African partners. But they won't do it. I think they are afraid that they will be out of a job, that they will be seen as unnecessary. I think they are just not trusting God. They are afraid to make the lower one as equipped as the higher one because they will be rubbing shoulders. They are afraid to rub shoulders."

9

As Joe and I finished our lunch, I said, "David's story saddened me. How is it that people can step forward in faith to serve the Lord, yet still be so fearful of change and uncertainty? And how could anyone who is representing the Lord and translating his word be concerned about status?"

"Well, we are just humans," Joe commented. "I see my own weaknesses and failures all the time. As a manager of a large staff, I can tell you that often I don't feel qualified, and I am always learning how to lead and how to do the job better. We are all on a journey. We just need to figure out how to bear with one another. Like your colleagues shared with you in the stories you've been telling me, we need to remember that God is doing more in each of us than we are doing for him. And we need to carry one another's burdens, or pain, as your friend Ruth put it. But, as it says in the book of Jude, Christ is faithful and will present us before his glorious presence, faultless and with great joy."

"That is amazing to think about. I often wonder about how we, the church, his bride, appear to him. And I need to remind myself that he will make us whole, he will heal our blemishes," I mused.

"I think it is interesting the way David expressed his concerns about the people he works with," I added. "He used some language that reminded me of something I had just read recently in the book of Zephaniah."

"The book of Zephaniah?" Joe said questioningly. "I'm not really that familiar with Zephaniah. What are you referring to?"

"Zephaniah was active during a time in Israel's history when the leadership and many of the people had turned away from God and were worshiping false gods. He warned the people of Judah that God's judgment would certainly come. He also warned some of the other surrounding nations that the 'Day of the Lord' was near, a time of wrath that would come as judgment on sin. But he also looked toward the future to a time of restoration. And here is what he said that I find interesting; and remember, he was speaking the words of

God; 'Then I will purify the lips of the peoples, that all of them may call on the name of the Lord and serve him shoulder to shoulder.'[7]

"The reason I find this so interesting is that it really reinforces for me what God is trying to do. He is building us up to be his people, a holy temple. He is building us up to work together in unity, shoulder to shoulder, as Zephaniah says, and as David put it so aptly. Naturally there is resistance as people learn to relinquish their plans and trust God. But the vision is one of a people who are united in Christ, who call on his name in sincerity, that idea of a pure lip, no deceit. And I think of Alice and how she became cognizant of how the Lord is doing more in her than she is doing for him, and Ruth's comment about the group carrying the pain together. These are pictures of his people who realize their dependence on God and go beyond common cultural responses, making an effort to respond to conflict according to what honors God.

"And just as it says in the first chapter of Zephaniah about that 'Day of the Lord,' human strength, human structures, and human resources are all worthless for protecting anyone from God's judgment. So people who have put their trust in anything but God will not escape judgment. That includes those trusting in other nations for protection or provision, trusting in some other god, even not recognizing God as the sovereign God who is involved in human affairs."

"Okay, so you are talking about even those who would claim to know God but live in a way that represents a sense of independence or self reliance, or maybe even those who have trusted in their own strength and wherewithal, like the mouse that managed to get himself out of the creamer." Joe was thinking about our prior conversation on Western man.

"Well, it's not me talking about it," I reminded him. "This is what the Scriptures say. This is what the prophets speaking for God say."

"I think a lot of people will be shocked on 'that day,'" Joe concluded.

"Yeah, probably so," I added ruefully.

"You know, in ancient times people always had some god or gods they were trusting in for one reason or another. But in modern times, especially with the philosophical ideas that have influenced Western culture and have found their way into the thinking of a lot of the rest of the world, people have turned to themselves as the makers of their destiny; they have become a god unto themselves. They have been strong-armed into believing that they must take God out of the equation if they are 'to survive,' as Nietzsche would put it, or 'confront their destiny with intentionality,' as Heidegger explains it.[8] In the long run, so much of this kind of thinking is just an attempt to escape the truth, to escape the God who sees and knows everything. Even those who still want to believe in God often do not believe that he is active in their individual lives. They are either unfamiliar with what God's Word says, do not trust what it says, or have simply forgotten what it says," I pointed out. "But that excuse will not redeem people from God's wrath on 'that day.' There will be no escape."

# 10

Joe and I both sat silent for a few minutes, each lost in our

own thoughts. My thoughts turned to family members and other

loved ones who had wandered from the truth or who had never

embraced the truth. I thought about the prophet Elijah when he

confronted the prophets of Baal, urging them to keep calling on their

god, mocking them and suggesting that they call louder in case he

was on a journey or needed to be awakened. He was angry; angry

that God's people had been so influenced by the opinions and ideas

of the pagan nations, and by the beliefs and behavior of their own

king Ahab of Judah, who himself had turned from God and done

more evil in the sight of the Lord than all the other kings who had

reigned before him. It made me angry, too, that our culture has been

so permeated by such ungodliness and has embraced foreign ideas

that came from ungodly philosophers and intellectuals. Even leaders

in the church promote some of these ideas, wrapping them in

culturally acceptable words that promise tolerance, partnership, compatibility, harmony, and intellectual reconciliation. I thought about the words from Zephaniah, the Lord's indictment against those in leadership in Jerusalem who were supposed to be preserving society but were contributing to its destruction.

Joe looked at me and said, "There is a lot of arrogance out there. A lot of pride, and a lot of contempt for those who believe in God's word."

"Yes, and according to what Zephaniah writes, all of that haughtiness and pride will be removed after the Lord's judgment on the nations. It says, 'But I will leave within you the meek and the humble.'[9] There will be a time of restoration when the Lord will remove the shame of his people; he will gather the outcasts and those who mourn for justice and righteousness and change their shame into praise." I was trying to imagine what that would be like.

I couldn't help but think about some of my colleagues who were such humble servants, doing the Lord's work in difficult places and under adverse circumstances.

"Joe, you know what is so amazing about some of my colleagues? They trust God even when there is conflict due to cultural differences, personality differences, misunderstandings, spiritual battles, uncertainties, and just general upheavals in life. They have learned that even though they make their plans and submit them to God, things don't always go as they might have thought. But they never give up hope or lose faith in him. They trust in Him, find refuge in him, and continue to serve him with gladness and joy, willing to wait for the day of restoration."

Joe and I talked for a while about the whole concept of serving the Lord, about the joy that should accompany such service, and about the sense of worship that becomes such an overwhelming presence when you are trusting the Lord and bringing all your needs to him.

"Joe, you know the story in the New Testament about some men who brought a paralytic to Jesus to be healed?"

"Sure. The house where Jesus was speaking was so crowded with people wanting to hear him that the men had to go up onto the roof and make a hole in it to lower the paralytic down in order to get him to Jesus." Joe was an avid reader of the New Testament and immediately found the story in the book of Mark.

"Well, I read something interesting, recently, in my Greek devotional about that story. In the Greek, you get the idea that the emphasis is not so much on the men but on their action. The men are bearing the paralytic to Jesus; the man is taken up by the four to Jesus, but they are unable to bring him to Jesus because of the crowd. The author of the reading points out that the word Mark uses for 'bringing' is used elsewhere in the gospels to show the act of 'offering' or 'presenting a gift' as an act of worship. And this same word is used in the Septuagint[10] in a sacrificial sense. The words stress the one to whom they are bringing him, Jesus. The author of the reading, a guy named David Wallace,[11] points out that the focus is not on the faith of the people but on bringing needs to Jesus, the one who has authority to heal and forgive, the one who deserves our worship. I appreciate the insights from those who grasp the Greek so well and turn up these kinds of theological gems."

"I see where you are going with this. So when we live in complete dependence on God, it is an act of worship." Joe had nailed it.

"I do believe so . . . I do believe so," I agreed.

"And when we look to other things to meet our needs we are failing to give due worship to the Lord," he surmised.

"I guess you could put it that way," I said thoughtfully.

We both needed to ponder that for a bit.

"That puts a whole new light on things for me," Joe said, shaking his head.

I agreed and recalled the times when I had looked to the things of the world to meet my needs rather than to the Lord.

Finally Joe broke the silence. "I think sometimes we need to clear our hearts and minds of the things of the world that crowd in and compete for our attention."

"Well, that is what God thinks, too, I believe." And I thought about Moses and what God had sent him to do for the Israelites who had been enslaved in Egypt.

*Part Three*

*That We May Worship the Lord*

*Journey Home*

*Three days they journeyed, three days they moved on.*
*He led them in rapture with heavenly song.*
*They crossed o'er that river, traversed Heaven's stream.*
*Together unfettered they worshiped their King.*
*With hearts overflowing they worshipped their King.*

## 11

*Moses was tending his father-in-law's flock of sheep out in the wilderness near Horeb, the mountain of God, when suddenly he saw a thorn bush that appeared to be on fire but was not being consumed by the fire. He walked closer to get a look at this incredible sight and as soon as he got close the Lord called to him from the bush. When Moses responded, the Lord told him not to come any closer and to remove his shoes because he was standing on holy ground. And there the Lord revealed himself to Moses as the God of Abraham, the God of Isaac, and the God of Jacob. Moses hid his face because he was afraid to look upon God. And God told Moses that he had heard the cries of his people who were enslaved in Egypt and now he was going to deliver them from that land by sending Moses to stand before Pharaoh and bring the sons of Israel out of there.*

*It was not what he would have chosen to do at this time in his life. He had become comfortable in the land of Midian, and he was getting on in years. Now he was being called to return to Egypt and bring God's people out of their slavery in that country. They had been there for four hundred years and God had heard their groaning and cries for help and he remembered his covenant with Abraham, with Isaac, and with Jacob. God had said to Moses, "Come, I will send you to Pharaoh that you may bring my people, the children of Israel, out of Egypt. You shall go to the king of Egypt and say to him, 'The Lord, the God of the Hebrews, has met with us; and now, please let us go a three days' journey into the wilderness, that we may sacrifice to the Lord our God.'" Yet, God also said he knew the king of Egypt would not allow it unless compelled by a mighty hand. God's plan was to strike Egypt with such wonders that the king would relent and allow them to leave, but only after having his heart hardened and then being struck by God's hand.*

*Moses had stood with his brother, Aaron, before Pharaoh. "Thus says the Lord, the God of Israel, 'Let my people go, that they may hold a feast to me in the wilderness.'" But Pharaoh answered, "Who is the Lord that I should obey him? I do not know the Lord and I will not let Israel go." Again they spoke to him saying, "The God of the Hebrews has met with us. Please let us go a three days' journey into the wilderness that we may sacrifice to the Lord our God..." And again they were turned away, and Pharaoh burdened the people with heavier labor because Moses wanted to take them from their work.*

*Moses and Aaron went again, and did as the Lord commanded. Aaron cast down his staff before Pharaoh and his servants, and it became a serpent and swallowed up the staffs that Pharaoh's wise men cast down in the same way, according to their secret arts. But Pharaoh's heart remained hardened just as the Lord had said.*

*The next morning Moses and Aaron went to Pharaoh again while he was standing on the bank of the Nile River. "The Lord, the God of the Hebrews, sent me to you, saying, 'Let my people go, that they may serve me in the wilderness. But so far, you have not obeyed.' Therefore the Lord says, 'This is how you will know that I am the Lord; with this staff I will strike the water in the Nile and it will turn to blood.'"*

*Again and again Moses went to Pharaoh saying, "Thus says the Lord, 'Let my people go, that they may serve me.'" And again and again Pharaoh's heart was hardened, and the Lord struck Egypt with plagues. The final plague was the death of all the firstborn in the land of Egypt, from the firstborn of Pharaoh to the firstborn of the captive in the dungeon; even the firstborn of all the livestock. All but the Israelites, whose doors were marked with blood, were struck with this final plague. After this, Pharaoh summoned Moses and Aaron and said, "Go out from here and serve the Lord, as you have said...be gone, and bless me also!"*

*And so God's people journeyed, and the Lord delivered them from their bondage and brought them out of the land of Egypt.*[12]

12

"I think we tend to forget the significance of what God did in bringing his people out of Egypt. You know, the people were admonished to remember the events leading up to their journey by celebrating the Passover meal every year. The Passover meal was their last meal in Egypt. Everything they were told to do in preparation for that meal and in the manner it was eaten was deeply symbolic. God wanted them to remember the significance of how he delivered them. And when they crossed through the body of water that God miraculously parted for them, arriving safely on the other shore after being pursued by Pharaoh's army, Moses and the people sang a song of victory, thanksgiving, and praise to the Lord."

"I know the basic story of Moses and the exodus," said Joe, "and I know there were some major issues that kept the Israelite people wandering in the desert for forty years. They did a lot of complaining, right?"

"It was also an issue of trust," I said. "God brought them into the desert to build a relationship of trust with them. He wanted them to acknowledge their dependence on him. It was to be a time of intimacy between them and God. Whenever they got to a place of need, they could call on him to provide and he would. The problem was that they kept forgetting, from one miraculous provision to another. When they were in need they complained bitterly and blamed Moses instead of looking to God and trusting him.

"In the Old Testament, God tells the prophet Hosea that in a future time he will lead his people into the desert again and it will be a time of true intimacy and peace between God and his people. In fact, he says that they will sing as in the day they came out of Egypt."

Joe had opened his Bible to the book of Hosea and was looking at some of the wording there. "I see what you mean," he said. "It also says he will remove the idolatry from among them, abolish all weapons of war; and here it says he will marry himself to them and they will know him intimately and acknowledge him.

Wow! That is quite a picture! And I get the impression that the intimacy comes from trust and a healthy sense of dependence on God, which is what we were talking about earlier when you mentioned the story of the men who brought the paralyzed man to Jesus…how that was an act of worship."

"It is really just incredible to think that our God has that kind of love for us," Joe reflected. "And I recall someplace else in the Bible that mentions that God will actually sing over his people. What do you know about that?"

"That is interesting that you bring it up; it is in the book of Zephaniah and in the New Testament in Revelation," I replied.

# 13

"Zephaniah tells of a day when God's people will worship him together without deceit or shame or fear of any enemies; when the Lord himself will live among his people. He will delight in them, calm their fears, and rejoice over them with joyful songs. He will bring them home and give them a name of distinction instead of disgrace."

"And what does it say in Revelation about singing?" Joe prompted.

"I think it is a beautiful fulfillment of the victory of God's people over everything that Egypt had represented as an idolatrous ruling nation that kept God's people in bondage and prohibited them from being able to know him and worship him. It says that all those who were victorious over the beast who had risen in the last days to deceive the people and lure them away from the truth were gathered together and they were singing the song of Moses and the song of the Lamb. Isn't that amazing?

"I think the song of the Lamb is probably the one that comes from chapter five in Revelation where the only one worthy to open the scroll that was sealed was the Lamb that had been slain. And when the Lamb came forward to take the scroll, the heavenly beings who gathered around the throne began to sing this song;

*You are worthy to take the scroll and break its seals and open it.*

*For you were slaughtered, and your blood has ransomed people for God from every tribe and language and people and nation.*

*And you have caused them to become a Kingdom of priests for our God, and they will reign on the earth.*

"Then, millions of the angels also began to sing this chorus;

*Worthy is the Lamb who was slaughtered –*

*to receive power and riches*

*and wisdom and strength*

*and honor and glory and blessing.*

"And then every creature in heaven and on earth and under the earth and in the sea sang,

*Blessing and honor and glory and power*

*Belong to the one sitting on the throne*

*And to the Lamb forever and ever.*[13]

Joe and I sat silently for a few minutes as we thought about the words from Revelation.

"So, the song of Moses and the song of the Lamb are significant because they are the combined songs of victory and worship and praise to God?" Joe asked.

"Yes, I think the idea is that God's glory and honor will have been restored through his people, and his mighty works will have been revealed to the nations and will result in awesome worship. It is a picture of God's people finally resting in all of his provisions and acknowledging complete dependence on him, but being joyful in that dependence and the victory that he has secured for them."

"That goes right back to what you were sharing the other day about people thinking that independence is so exemplary," Joe added.

"It depends on what your dependence or independence are related to. I think people who have worked hard and tried not to be dependent on the government can end up with a sense of independence that also shuts God out. But it is just as dishonoring to God when people fail to look to God to supply and become dependent on other sources to his exclusion. God uses many sources to meet people's needs, but they need to remember he is the one to look to and bring their needs to him first, like the men who brought the paralytic to Jesus."

"So, when God brought his people out of Egypt, they initially rejoiced and sang a victory song acknowledging that God had delivered them. But then they got to a place where they were in need and failed to trust him, right?" Joe voiced.

"Yes, but God provided and kept pursuing the relationship. It's just that time and time again they complained and displayed a lack of trust and constantly blamed Moses for everything. Finally, when they were so close to the Promised Land, they had still not learned to trust God."

"So that is why they ended up another forty years in the desert until a new generation rose up, and then God allowed them to move forward and cross the Jordon into the land he had promised, the land he was giving them as a home." Joe completed my thoughts.

"Well, one day God will lead us in that victory song of Moses and of the Lamb and bring us to our ultimate home. Like the Bible says, we are sojourners on this earth," I added.

"I guess the song from back in the Exodus account has an underlying meaning and message that will be applicable to us on that day. And the words from the song of the Lamb shed light on the events that took place on the night of the Passover when the blood from the lamb was put on the doors of the people of Israel so the angel of death would not strike any of them. It reflects the ultimate victory and salvation for God's people." Joe read the words from Revelation,

> *For you were slaughtered, and your blood has ransomed*
> *people for God from every tribe and language and people*
> *and nation.*
> *And you have caused them to become a Kingdom of priests*
> *for our God, and they will reign on the earth.[14]*

Then we both looked again at the words of the song of Moses and the people, after they crossed through the waters and were safe on the other side and the Egyptian army that had pursued them was

swept into the sea. . .

# 14

*"I will sing to the LORD, for he is highly exalted. The horse and its rider he has hurled into the sea. The LORD is my strength and my song; he has become my salvation. He is my God, and I will praise him, my father's God, and I will exalt him. The LORD is a warrior; the LORD is his name. Pharaoh's chariots and his army he has hurled into the sea. The best of Pharaoh's officers are drowned in the Red Sea. The deep waters have covered them; they sank to the depths like a stone. Your right hand, O LORD, was majestic in power. Your right hand, O LORD, shattered the enemy. In the greatness of your majesty you threw down those who opposed you. You unleashed your burning anger; it consumed them like stubble. By the blast of your nostrils the waters piled up. The surging waters stood firm like a wall; the deep waters congealed in the heart of the sea. The enemy boasted, 'I will pursue; I will overtake them. I will divide the spoils; I will gorge myself on them. I will draw my sword and my hand will destroy them.' But you blew with your breath, and*

*the sea covered them. They sank like lead in the mighty waters. Who among the gods is like you, O LORD? Who is like you-- majestic in holiness, awesome in glory, working wonders? You stretched out your right hand and the earth swallowed them. In your unfailing love you will lead the people you have redeemed. In your strength you will guide them to your holy dwelling. The nations will hear and tremble; anguish will grip the people of Philistia. The chiefs of Edom will be terrified, the leaders of Moab will be seized with trembling, the people of Canaan will melt away; terror and dread will fall upon them. By the power of your arm they will be as still as a stone-- until your people pass by, O LORD, until the people you bought pass by. You will bring them in and plant them on the mountain of your inheritance-- the place, O LORD, you made for your dwelling, the sanctuary, O Lord, your hands established. The LORD will reign for ever and ever."[15]*

"After something as amazing and miraculous as God parting the waters of the sea and enabling his people to go through to the other side, you would think his people would have no trouble trusting him through the desert in all the difficulties there," Joe shook his head in disbelief.

"I guess we all tend to forget how mighty God is and how much he just wants us to trust him in all things, even when the circumstances seem insurmountable," I agreed.

"And that is why he was constantly telling his people to remember all the things he had done," Joe added.

"We should not forget. . .we have God's written word with all the stories of what he has done to restore us and bring us back into a right relationship with him, one where we can freely worship him and know him intimately." But I knew that his Word also says that many will remain in their hard-hearted condition and refuse to look to him.

# 15

"Will they remember?" Joe and I wondered as we looked at some verses. I remembered the words from the book of Revelation, "Blessed are those who hear the word of God and take to heart what is written in it."[16]

From Daniel we read, "Many will be purified, made spotless and refined, but the wicked will continue to be wicked. None of the wicked will understand, but those who are wise will understand."[17] From Hosea we read, "Who is wise? He will realize these things. Who is discerning? He will understand them."[18] From Revelation we read, "The time is near. Let him who does wrong continue to do wrong; let him who is vile continue to be vile; let him who does right continue to do right; and let him who is holy continue to be holy."[19]

We thought about many verses in the Scriptures that remind us that God is the one who directs our steps and guards our souls, and our victory is in him. "In all these things we are triumphantly victorious due to the one who loved us."[20]

We thought about the fact that God knows every hair on our head and is intimately involved in every aspect of our lives. We have not been left alone to manage our way through this world. "We know that if the earthly tent we live in is torn down, we have a building in heaven that comes from God, an eternal house not built by human hands" (2 Corinthians 5:1).[21]

We were comforted to think that he will ultimately lead us home and rejoice over us with singing. Our dependence on him is true worship. "Blessed is the man who trusts in the Lord, whose confidence is in him. He will be like a tree planted by the water that sends out its roots by the stream. It does not fear when heat comes; its leaves are always green. It has no worries in a year of drought and never fails to bear fruit."[22] "Trust in the Lord with all your heart and lean not on your own understanding; in all your ways acknowledge him, and he will make your paths straight."[23]

*Sing, O Daughter of Zion; shout aloud, O Israel! Be glad and rejoice with all your heart, O Daughter of Jerusalem! The LORD has taken away your punishment; he has turned back your enemy. The LORD, the King of Israel, is with you; never again will you fear any harm.*

*Zephaniah 3:14-15[24]*


*Great and amazing are your deeds, O Lord God the Almighty! Just and true are your ways, O King of the nations! Who will not fear, O Lord, and glorify your name? For you alone are holy. All nations will come and worship you, for your righteous acts have been revealed.*

*Revelation 15:3-4[25]*

# EPILOGUE

## 2015

### *Beginnings*

*Many people do not believe in a literal understanding of creation. Science has become their god and they have been enticed away from the truth. Oh, some may say they believe that God created everything by his Word, just as it says in the very first chapter of Genesis, and as it is reaffirmed in the first three verses of the Gospel of John. But then they waver; they reason; they look to their own understanding. Perhaps they do not understand the integrity of the spoken word when it is spoken in truth. Yes, the spoken word. It is powerful. Jesus himself testified that the words he spoke were truth. He also said that everyone would be held accountable for every careless word spoken (Matthew 12:16). Would Jesus have affirmed the creation of one man and one woman?*

*Would he have misled his disciples regarding the truth of the account of Noah and the flood (Hebrews 11:7, 2 Peter 2:4)? Would he have allowed his disciples to believe that the universe was created at God's command (Hebrews 11:3, 2 Peter 3:5-6), that Enoch was taken and did not experience death (Hebrews 11:5)?*

*No, it is we ourselves that pervert the spoken word. We use it to deceive, and we are deceived by it. But one day we will have a pure lip; we will not speak with deception (Zephaniah 3:9,13). The truth will prevail.*

### What is Truth?

*"But, what is truth? Why would people want to evade it?"*

*"Long ago someone else asked the same question, 'What is truth?'"*

*"Who was that?"*

"A very powerful political figure during Jesus' last days, Pontius Pilate. And now in these days, because of greed and corruption, we see a similar disdain for absolute truth. Pilate's question may have been sincere, but his actions testify to his partiality toward pleasing the masses.

"Will you tell that story?"

"I will start it . . . but that is another story for another time. It is the cosmic clash between two kingdoms that are still at war to this day."


People weren't hungry for truth. No, they were hungry for revenge. Truth was irrelevant. But if those in power could simply provide entertainment and the occasional crumbs of pseudo-justice to pacify their blood lust, the masses could be appeased. In fact, if the masses could be appeased so easily, they could be as easily swayed to cast their vote for that which favored their lusts rather *than the truth. For what is truth but that which is in the*

*eye of the beholder. There is no absolute truth, right?*

[1] 1 Enoch is an ancient text of prophetic sayings attributed to Enoch, son of Jared, as recorded in Genesis 5:18. In the New Testament, the book of Jude, verse 14 refers to a quote from Enoch.

[2] From Oswald Chambers' devotional, My Utmost for His Highest.

[3] From Edward Hall's book, Beyond Culture.

[4] *Culture, Leadership, and Organizations: The GLOBE Study of 62 Societies.*

[5] John Steinbeck's novel, Of Mice and Men, portrays existence without the hope of God. He takes the title from a poem by Robert Burns, To A Mouse, which also implies a world where fate is in control.

[6] The article, Ezekiel's Rhetoric: Ancient Near Eastern Building Protocol and Shame and Honor as the Keys in Identifying the Builder of the Eschatological Temple, can be found in the Journal of the Evangelical Theological Society, volume 56, number 4, page 707.

[7] Zephaniah 3:9 New International Version (NIV).

[8] See R.C. Sproul's book, The Consequences of Ideas, for more on the philosophers that influenced Western thinking in an ungodly direction.

[9] Zephaniah 3:12 NIV.

[10] The Septuagint is the Greek version of the Old Testament.

[11] Wallace's article, Jesus Heals the Paralytic, is found in Devotions on the Greek New Testament.

[12] Taken from Exodus chapters 3 through 14.

[13] Revelation 5:9-13, New Living Translation (NLT)

[14] Revelation 5:9-10, NLT

[15] Exodus 15:1-18, NIV

[16] Revelation 1:3, International Standard Version

[17] Daniel 12:10, NIV

[18] Hosea 14:9, NIV

[19] Revelation 22:11, NIV

[20] Romans 8:37, International Standard Version (ISV)

[21] 2 Corinthians 5:1, ISV

[22] Jeremiah 17:7, NIV

[23] Proverbs 3:5, NIV

[24] NIV

[25] English Standard Version (ESV)

# About the Author

Dr. MARGARET DOLL serves with Wycliffe Bible Translators and the Summer Institute of Linguistics as a media consultant and is the Resource Coordinator and Associate International Coordinator for International Media Services. She holds a Master of Divinity and Doctor of Ministry in Leadership from Gordon-Conwell Theological Seminary. Her doctoral thesis includes oral strategies for leadership training in oral societies.

Made in the USA
Charleston, SC
27 February 2016